ONENESS

Principles of
World Peace

ONENESS
Principles of World Peace

Copyright © 2015 by Brian Scott Baskins
www.brianscottbaskins.com
www.globalunitymedia.com

All rights reserved. No part of this book may be reproduced or transmitted in any form or by any means, electronic or mechanical, including photocopying, recording, or by any information storage retrieval system, without the written permission of the publisher, except where permitted by law.

Cover Design by Lillian De Jesus, Tigerlily Virtual Assistance

Author Photograph by Chance Hammock

ISBN-13: 978-1-942468-00-4

LCCN: 2015900372

Global Unity Media
Washington, DC

Page

Table of Contents

Chapter

Introduction i
1. The Maze of Racial and National Identity 1
2. Authority 9
3. Idea 13
4. Identification 17
5. Identification with the Idea of Race 19
6. Genetics 29
7. Culture 31
8. Dropping the Maze of Racial and National Identity 35
9. Freedom 37
10. Self-knowledge 39
11. Racial and National Discord 41
12. Process and Progress 45
13. Realization 47
14. Individualized Expression 49
15. Global Unity 51
Afterword 55

Introduction

Can You Hear the Messenger's Cry?

Dear Reader, please answer this heartfelt question: "How do you experience global unity?"

Where do you go or what must you do to have it? Can you get a degree from a university majoring in global unity? Can you buy some global unity at the store or maybe order it as an entrée cooked "medium well" at a restaurant? Does anyone have the authority or credentials to confer it to another?

Who do you need to be to see the obvious and try to show it to another, to put the feeling of what has been clearly seen into words, to communicate and confer it to a reader? You only need to look for yourself, not look to another to explain it to you. You can either see the fact, or you don't. No one else can see for you. The only authority in global unity comes with the facts your own heart has seen.

The Message of Global Unity represents an objective, scientific approach that solves the problem of the consequences of racial and national identification, a mistaken identity. The perception of your essential bond is your unchanging connection and permanent relationship to all of humanity. This correction in your identity ends separation and leaves isolation behind, as you see the truth that you are forever related in an entirely different way than mere ancestral or familial ties.

The dimension of global unity is real and already going on right now if your inward action and being are in alignment with it. You see yourself and all others in a different light. Are you capable of experiencing global unity? Its freedom immediately opens to you through your individual perception. In case you would enjoy a little help, I am going to show you global unity through six central principles to consider when investigating global unity:

1. Self-Knowledge--is the "how to" or personal way of removing the inward impediments, barriers, and ideological escapes that prevent global unity's expression.

2. Simply Seeing--starts with observing the verbal husk that you are not—conditioning.

3. Conditioning Projects as Discord--events or experiences denoting racial or national conflict.

4. Realization--the first moment you profoundly detect yourself as human awareness—the listening and looking part of you that is identical to all humanity.

5. Individual Expression--you express global unity. Once you are free to see what unites humanity, you can easily show others.

6. Global Unity is Freedom--the state or abiding sense that the looking and listening part of you (and everybody on the planet) obviously has no part of racial or national identification.

    1. Self-knowledge provides a "how to" technique for attaining global unity. It dispels illusions and shows the psychological causes where human conflict lurks. Self-knowledge is creative problem solving. You are thinking strategically—outside the box. Through observing the mental stumbling blocks and assumptions that hamper global unity, you are free to move beyond traditional thinking patterns and conventional behaviors. You transcend conformity and your resistance to change.

    "What is global unity? What is it not?" Can you find the inward turning point on which freedom hinges? What is the exact nature and content of the problem? Why has racial, national and cultural identification become so important as a continuous preoccupation for mankind? When you simply observe racial and national identity as conditioning, you see it displays as racial discord and war, two sides of the same coin. The sudden disclosure that you are in a maze brings release. You realize that the only way out of the maze is to jump and go beyond the impediment of false identification.

    Self-knowledge starts the journey in the dimension of global unity when the individual watches identification move as conditioning. Consciously doing the listening and looking aspect of simple seeing is a voyage of direct contact with being human awareness. Self-knowledge leads the way to freedom, yet the beginning is the same as the end. The same objective, impartial attention you pay in observing conditioning and its effects as racial and national discord, is the second principle, which I call "simply seeing."

2. Simply seeing is the only way to discover your true being as human awareness through doing "simple seeing" of the verbal husk and conditioned thinking process that conceals it. Consciously doing the listening and looking part that you are, is your timeless link to all others. Simply seeing is the missing piece that completely ends any sense of difference through the individual insight there is only the identical, the one thing of human awareness.

Humanity is already one thing: united in the nature and structure of its essence. Being in touch with your true nature as human awareness, you see exactly what action constitutes humanity being one thing.

3. Conditioning Projects as Discord. By understanding the entire destructive process of an illusory sense of self (based on identification with the idea of race or nationality) you see the whole structure of racial and national discord, both its generally unseen, yet audible causes as well as its catastrophic effects. As you observe your so-called race, nationality and culture as mere programming and environmental influences, be aware of the words being said, the stream of thoughts that give meaning, significance, value and importance to these objects of observation.

How much emphasis do you invest in these objects, and your superficial physical description or surface attributes? Are they all-important? Do they call for verbal or violent defense if criticized or denounced? Would a series of front-page news articles maligning the group you falsely identify with upset you? To the degree this is true, is the degree of your infection with the contagion of racial and national identity.

It is also the degree to which you are responsible for the human conflict in the world. The people who are fighting, feel the same as you do. The same mental impetus or cause, illusory or not, will inevitably result in the same effects. Why should you identify with the idea of nationality, race or culture at all? Oh, to explore and find out first-hand the attributes and qualities of human awareness! This discovery of being human awareness is called realization.

4. Realization releases you from the separating maze of racial and national identity. This key principle just means you can see it right now with your own eyes because you have the freedom to go beyond conditioning. Your new perspective is like an ever-present lens changing the way you see things. You have the vision of human awareness.

Your individual authentic experiencing of your own identity as human awareness, as simple seeing, is instantaneous global unity. For when you see what you genuinely are, you also see what every human being is and that you are never different, other than, separate or apart. This union you discover for yourself through actually being human awareness, which is to simply see.

Being has its own doing, they go together, you cannot have one without the other: they are one thing. Can you do passive, receptive and unconditioned watching? To be human awareness is to do what human awareness does, which is a simple, relaxed non-verbal seeing. What a passionate and engaged simple seer can do to inform, and encourage is boundless through individual initiative and expression.

5. Individual Expression. Global unity springs into action individually. How do you "do" global unity? On every day of the year, there is something going on in the world that could use the heightened perception of global unity, the profound feeling of already being one thing. Your newfound discovery makes you useful and helpful. Life is full of new purpose. Your interests and concerns are not separate and apart from one another.

The earth is becoming technologically global in nature, yet remains without the understanding necessary to bring about the cooperation needed to avoid tearing the planet into pieces. *The Message of Global Unity* highlights the importance of humanity's realistic true nature, not just to underpin world peace, but to personally weave the fabric of global society through individual action. You are free to implement your new insight.

6. Global Unity is Freedom. Release from the maze of fictitious identification makes you able or free to begin your own authentic journey into the dimension called global unity. Freedom lies in the impartial observation of the factor that binds. True liberation from national and racial identification begins with the simple notice of the impeding conditioning though self-knowledge. You must first be inwardly free

from all the causes of racism and nationalism, to be "free at last." Racial discord is nothing but the result and projection of the false racial identities society is held within.

There is no real freedom from racism without discarding the idea of racial and national identity. Only the individual can find freedom from the psychological fetters of a false sense of separation and difference from one another. Can you go beyond this limitation? Can you break through and leave this odious burden behind? Can you bring about true change inwardly, a psychological revolution that makes a real difference in your daily living and actions through perceiving yourself and all others as you really are? It is entirely up to you, the reader taking this journey.

By understanding what one truly is, your essential, primary nature as human awareness, global unity naturally and easily comes into being. When humanity's timeless true nature is acknowledged and explored freely and individually, that feeling of being separate and apart dissolves and vanishes. Be a witness as racial and national discord crumbles!

So. What do you consider yourself? The Messenger's cry is "I am what you are!" The real essence of humanity allows for no dissension or discord. Global unity is launched with your freedom and ability to see that humanity is already one thing.

1. The Maze of Racial and National Identity

"Understanding the whole process of the content, nature and structure of racial discord which is the conditioned brain's identification with the idea of race, is the beginning of true freedom from racism."

The well-dressed woman had an impressive collection of jewelry. She identified with it, for it was important to her, it made her feel like herself. She had many, many memories that she was fond of, and wearing the jewelry reminded her of the past and so she cherished it. She wanted to remember and so would adorn herself with all kinds of jewelry, for she really loved it all. But then life suddenly changed. The actual facts were different and it began with an allergic reaction to nickel but eventually metallic jewelry of any kind against her skin caused her to break out in fiercely inflamed pustules. The red sores were an adornment she could do without. But she did not want people to think she was doing poorly, so she had taken to carrying an assortment of jewelry in a box, matching whatever ensemble she had on at the time. If anyone spent more than thirty seconds speaking with her, even complete strangers, out would trot the box.

SA: "I cannot wear jewelry anymore, but I used to love wearing it. This is what I would have worn today. What do you think of it? Isn't it lovely?"

In this way, she added more experience to her identification with being something permanent mentally that wore jewelry. Even when it was obviously harmful she couldn't let it go, just like those adorned with the costume jewelry of racial, cultural and national identification.

She was not free. Thinking that her identification with the idea of race had some great meaning and importance, she talked about it endlessly; everything was referenced by it. She would seek out and attend events where she felt her kind was not wanted, feeling certain that her kind was not wanted just because they were not there. She thought, "they don't want us here, or more of us would be here." When informed of or invited to any social occasion, she always wondered if there were to be any other orange people there, and just how many, and went to see if they were "acting orange" to the satisfaction of her definition of "orangeness".

Race was her criterion for deciding if something was worthwhile or merited her participation and support. She inquired at the bookstore for the "orange-nation" book or magazine section for she only read "orange" books, watched "orange" movies, attended "orange" churches and visited "orange" websites. She was completely contained within her self-created and self-sustained prison of "orange" identity. This was her conditioning, for she accepted as true what she had been told, and it was now her habitual way of thinking and feeling. She reveled in the narrowness of nationalism with the bias of bigotry, which carried with it the pride and shame of racial identification.

Conformity was conventionality and her racial identity was born of simplistic tradition. She wanted to enhance and expand the culture of her race by dwelling upon its history and traditions. She wanted to counter the negative images promoted in the media, which she felt her group neither reported, owned nor managed. She was saturated with the sickening self-seeking of racial solidarity, where the only political and social causes she espoused were along orange lines. She was completely unaware of what she was, so was always trying to become something else, what she would "like" to be. She liked all her "used to bes", all the things she remembered about herself, and so she was always identifying with activities that would add to them.

She was identified with race and all that she knew had happened to hers and was still happening. She needed it to happen because her identification must feed on repeated experience--it must always be adding to itself, trying to maintain its permanency. She projected her inner state by stealthily defacing symbolic places with slogans attacking her own racial identity. She must have these incidents! Depending on these experiences confirmed her mirage and fed her identification through manifestation, for the inner must become the outer.

SA: "I ask every orange male child what they want to become as they grow up, and they all say 'athletes.' If that is not conditioning, I don't know what is! I want my kids to have something else in mind to avoid the tremendous disappointment that is coming if they don't find something else of value and significance to do."

She could see that wanting to be an athlete included allowing living locomotives to crash into each other for entertainment. There was great compensation involved for one must be compensated for one's bodily injuries. A body in constant pain colors all of one's experience: you cannot forget about it, it is always there. The organism might then seek escape from sleeplessness through the overuse of painkillers with its rapacious ravaging of one's liver, aging and further dulling the organism, distorting perception unto death. She did not want that for her orange boys.

She wanted to "gather together" separate groups of humans and promoted something called, "racial harmony" even though such a thing was as likely, as possible, as "obedient cats." She was very proud of her background and the resilience of her ancestors, yet she lamented the lack of "orange unity". She could not understand why all those who were also orange could not join together, and be a strong social, economic and political force. She felt that her people had been "divided and conquered" and she lamented the endless bickering and infighting. She felt urgency, for she knew she had to be "twice as good to go half as far," even though others claimed she did half as much to get twice as far. She was completely unaware there can be never be true human unity based upon a fictitious identity, for the real cannot be founded on the false but only on facts. Anything less will falter, fall, and fail.

SA: "I know I am orange because when I look in the mirror, I see orange. The legacy, history and pride of my race are very important to me. Racial violence is merely routine and I am not in the least bit interested in global unity."

BB: "What sees this objective phenomenon, or the facts of your superficial physical and cultural attributes? Only that which you are: human awareness. As you set aside your ancestor worship and the belief that you are what they thought they were, a member of a race or nation, there is the beginning of freedom. Seeing orange is unrelated to ideas about it, much less identification with those ideas. Identification illegitimately uses racial and national ideas, so that the mind can become something permanent. The 'not me' gives importance to the 'me'. Identification says that some labels are good and others evil; some are 'not like me' and some are 'like me.' "

SA: "We don't need this self-knowledge approach to global unity. It is too obscure and difficult. We just need to do better. We should make a point to accept and value the differences in people. We must recognize that we all come from different backgrounds and have different life experiences. Specifically, we should have a little more patience and just be a little more forgiving of others. If only for the children."

BB: "Bigotry is a psychological ailment, not merely a social or economic one. Through intelligence you see that racial and national identity is ill-fitting, uncomfortable and absurd. Racial and national identity is also not congruent to a child's experiencing their best individual realization of global unity."

SA: "I begin to see now that racial and national identity, or any identification of any sort whatsoever, are not conducive to global unity. To identify is to be caught up in pretense and not the felt presence of human awareness. An identity based upon the confused idea of race or nationality is to be incomplete, to be divided, fragmentary and in conflict with others. An identity based on what you really are is all inclusive, it allows for no diversity. Where there is global unity, diversity has no meaning or importance for there is only one thing, human awareness, not two or more things to be reconciled. But shamefully, I am still preoccupied by questions along the lines of 'what's in global unity for me? What can I get out of it?'"

BB: "This awareness of your true nature simply leaves no room for the false conditioning of national and racial identity. Your true identity as awareness does not do anything for you. There is nothing "you" can get out of "it." Reality is not for gratification of your desires or avoidance of your fears. It is not about pleasure, but merely seeing the naked facts as they are and being in touch with Reality. You want to see and intend to look. This is a serious hunger and interest to earnestly see obvious facts very clearly, without depending upon the authority of anyone else. When you come to this realization of your true identity, something as inadequate and partial as racial and cultural identity is seen as superfluous and discarded. This realization naturally, inevitably, demands global unity. The sense of global unity comes not by force, but through the unstructured spontaneity and unorganized movement of freedom.

"Preoccupation with the past through thinking about it absorbs and robs the organism of the energy of human awareness. The mental activity is unceasing because it is derived from identification with the idea of being the thinker. To complete drop the label, you must end completely, totally, the labeler, the identification with thinking, words and the labyrinth of the lies of language. You are deeply involved in your psychological reactions, so there is very little alert and silent watching and listening. Thinking, or psychological language, appears to be the exclusive activity of what you are. But memory and thinking are plainly mere capacities of human awareness. Thinking in terms of the idea of race, breeds a sense of separation, which in turn brings with it its own hate, jealousy and fear.

"It insults intelligence that your primary essence is associated with an invalid and meaningless word called race. Once you clearly see its immaturity and danger, it is discarded like any other childhood fantasy. When you encounter explanations of racial identity, you must remain tolerant and smile upon it, as the childish thing that it is. Nothing seems more ignorant, superstitious and absurd. True tolerance is born of the compassion in noticing how the unintelligent, unaware and unconscious cling to racial and national identification and thrash about in the enclosure of its maze."

* * *

Can an individual's essence be found in chromosomes, semen, in hormones, in the egg or DNA? Are you the skin, the pigment, the facial features, the hair texture or color? Is that really, truly, actually you? Or are you merely aware of these simple facts, you perceive and see them? The stupidity of your distinctions and separations are clearly seen: your bodily jewelry, decorations, adornments and cultural ornaments are seen to have very little meaning, if any at all. Your true nature is not found in the costume jewelry of color, culture or chromosome. These factors are only counterfeit charms on links connected in a shackle of dissension and strife. Obsession with the texture of your hair, a natural universal excrescence, is as different from and completely unrelated to the treasure of what you truly are as fingernails or body odor.

* * *

Although their personal hygiene went neglected, the pirates kept the vessel spotless to not ruin or damage their cargo or allow vermin to flourish. After swabbing the deck, they rinsed the filthy mops in a wooden pail of salty seawater. No matter how many times they changed the water, the dirt held in the matted strands of the mop was so great that the clear water in the pail turned into cloudy, muddy hues. Small things were easily lost on a ship with the constant movement of the waves, the wind, and the criminal class one traveled with, for he was an orchid pirate. He and his colleagues did not spare much time for ablutions or on grooming the hair on their faces and heads. Their straight crown and facial hair grew long. After a while, the long hair would grow into a tangled thick mass. They found that if they twisted small valuables into their matted hair, they could better keep up with them and keep their eyes on them. Precious gems, coins, anything small might find its way there. Fungal infections were common, and the pirate's life was hard, but not harder than the lives of the green slaves they observed and traded on distant islands.

The green slaves saw the pirates too and marveled. Many of the slaves had just arrived, and they had never witnessed such a peculiar appearance. The slaves were from a region where the sun scorched. Fiery climates made matted hairstyles maladaptive and unintelligent, as they held too much heat in the body, causing dehydration and death. It was climatically impossible! Sweat-filled matted hair also drew swarms of tormenting insects and so it was simply not done.

The orchid pirate's hair was the original dreadlock. This convention was obviously too hot for those residing in the region of the green slaves' birth to wear. But it was cooler on the islands, surrounded by brilliant blue water, with constant trade winds blowing off the open seas, and hurricanes. Some of the green slaves soon adopted the orchid pirates' hairstyle. They let their hair grow long into a twisted mass of matted tendrils. Centuries went by, erasing origins, and in a region northerly of the islands, millions of so-called descendants of green slaves were proudly wearing an orchid pirate hairstyle, thinking it was derived from the land of their green ancestor's birth. But it was not!

Oh, the absurdity of racial identification when your emblem of racial solidarity, actually wholly originated from outside your so-called race, belonging entirely to another! See the stupidity and lowliness of your intelligence to even debate such a thing, giving significance to a hairstyle and humanity's surrender to strand unmanageability. Can you see how easy it is to get a rise out of someone when identification transforms a trivial fact into something important enough to defend? Even the most ludicrous story can provoke defensiveness where identification is present. See the insanity of racial identification, which gives undue importance to superficial excrescences and adornments, for in what you really are, there is no difference whatsoever. Racial identity is a broad, vague nonsense where you emphasize the characteristics that fit, or should be, and utterly fail to notice all those qualities that do not. Your decorations are a very transparent attempt to seem really different. The captivity of racial and national identity relies on appearing different from what is in essence identical to you.

When your cultural conditioning and varying superficial physical attributes are seen in their rightful place they can no longer serve any destructive purpose. Once superficial physical attributes and culture are depersonalized; they are simply seen as objective, impartial, scientific facts about you. You no longer feel ownership or protective of them, so there is no self-defensiveness. You no longer nurture, emphasize, or amplify these facts: you are just aware of them. You are no longer "located" there, attached to or identified with any of the objects within what you truly are, that simple seeing as human awareness. Instead you freely and thoroughly study, examine, and explore the nature, qualities, attributes and features of awareness.

2. Authority

Authority is a snare, and prevents freedom. Your conditioned mind is always the comfortable, conventional modes of thinking. The contents by which you are manipulated are by ideas or creations of the closed mind. The mental illusions and manufactured conceptions are the comments and contemporary climate of your belief. The conditioning of the 18th century persists today in the archaic classification of humans into races. The conditioning of nationalism and culturalism surfaced long before, where the self-centeredness of the individual extended to the group.

Pride in your parentage and heritage is not global unity, but a mere obsession and preoccupation with poisonous precepts passed on by your parents, a pestilence from the past. The greatest feat of racists was the insidious introduction, spread and acceptance of the absurd idea of race: that it had any meaning, value, importance or significance whatsoever. What followed was the assumption that racial identity represented something real and factual, that it had worth, usefulness, and was true. What serpent of language slid by and told you that you were naked, that you had a race, or a nationality? How do you know, without having accepted authority? Regardless of who told you were green, or of a nation, your reaction to this assertion or suggestion was identification. You are completely convinced of nothing more than a theory, a concept and idea by so-called authorities.

We are selective of our authorities, choosing only the ones that support our illusions. What you truly are, has no color, it is simply aware of all color. The perception of color must be seen as merely a fact. It is beautiful to look at any hue. Only awareness contains all colors and all colors are seen only by awareness. What does this imply regarding superficial skin tone differences?

Have you ever noticed how, when you are not preoccupied, you encounter art and there is a sense of great beauty? The beauty lies not in the colored paint, the canvas, the lighting or even the poorly hidden security cameras, but as an aspect of what you really are, of human awareness. There is beauty in the looking, in the awareness of any color. But the introduction of the psychological process, (of a mental and emotional dependency or need surrounding a pigment), associates chromatic shading with the idea of a race you belong to and must therefore defend. This is a very ugly thing.

The perception of the beauty of a rose is one thing. But holding on to the rose as a pleasurable experience, gripping it tightly as something you feel is important and involved in your sense of self, of wanting to defend and protect the rose, you find your hand pierced with thorns and your feet strewn with lifeless petals. The beauty of the rose is destroyed through attachment and possessiveness. Whether it is a rose or the idea of race, the identification process changes it from a mere objective perception, to something worth killing over. Corpses strangely lose their race with the distortion of decay and decomposition-related color changes. They were just a dead human, not a death belonging to a race or nation.

You have accepted an opinion without questioning its value and implications. You conform to convention and learn to agree on the realness of an idea, which gives it existence, or history. Just because something has existence, a psychological history in the mind of man as conditioning, does not mean it is real or factual. This history is then relentlessly reiterated to each generation as the conditioning of racial and national identity. The idea of race creates discord and confusion by merely comparing one fact to another, and comparison, like choice, can only arise as an outcome of conditioning.

You have given up the clarity of your own insight to the assumptions, conclusions, and opinions of others, or what you have been told or taught, which comprise your conditioning. You have blindly accepted the assertions and statements of others. When racial and national identity is now ceded to be inaccurate, false and wholly misunderstood, you then proceed to global unity, where all humans embrace the one thing that they truly are, essentially. You no longer rely on the authority of "leaders" to escape from your personal, individual responsibility to express and expand global unity. Then, differences seen are only between an individual's and another's degree of awareness, but not in all of humanity being human awareness.

Racial identity is nothing more than traditional opinion. You have been conditioned to accept the idea of race as a basis of your essential quality or nature. Holding on to racial and national identification is the willingness to be society's fool, having been taught or told this sheer nonsense. Examine this and see how artificial and immature racial identity is for yourself. No matter what experiences you have in life, it will always happen within what you really are, human awareness.

Nothing can change that. Clearly seeing this, you no longer value or give any importance, significance or meaning whatsoever to superficial physical and cultural differences.

All of humanity's accomplishments through history came out of human awareness, which is a new basis of personal worth and well-being. You instantly lay claim to every innovation, invention or insight because it all came out of and resides within that very same thing that defines all of humanity. Once you have this sense of there being no difference between human beings, you are also freed from all racial and national pride, envy, guilt or shame.

You cannot behold or see anything in the material world of form without it being a part of you, for it is within what you really are, human awareness. All is inside of you. Everything in life, the whole of life, depends upon awareness, for there is nothing that exists that is separate or apart from it. Racial discord and dissension, or disorder, exist within the order of awareness, as conditioning. That is the first and last cause of racial and national dissension; your identification, attachment and clinging to the idea of race or nationality.

3. Idea

What of the idea of race? Racial identity is mere attachment to an idea. It is but an educated guess, a destructive psychological process and conditioned speculation accepted as real and natural and given inordinate significance. Racial identification includes all the images and ideas of what is means to be a race, all the associated "should bes" and "should nots". It is viewed as something essential and worthwhile as if it conveys something of inherent value. See the utter nonsense of this. There is no reason, especially in light of the urgency of global threats and gene science that this divisive opinion should continue.

When you use the idea or word "race", it is used to convey what feeling? Is there the feeling of its being a generic description, or its being the inherent nature and structure of another, as different from your own? Just as the word "tree" translated into any and every language is not and can never actual be a tree, just as an exhaustive sixty-six volume encyclopedia about trees is not a tree, so also be skeptical when what is being said uses words such as "I, me, my, mine, myself." The description of a thing is never actually that thing. No description can capture what you truly are; it has no quality that one can name. It is not the ugly, destructive thing of all racial and nationalistic identification.

The technical and proper place and function of race is as a mere social convenience, to describe, distinguish or categorize various phenotypes or superficial physical attributes. But you have been conditioned, told to conform, trained to be molded to your identification with the idea of race. Given the extraordinary importance race, culture and nationalism are given by society, it is staggering to truly grasp its smallness and lack of meaning. Its significance wanes even more when you see it is but a verbal description compared to the complete totality and whole being of what you are.

Have you ever felt the discontent that comes from racial or national identities? Have you ever caught that intimation that all identifications are false and that you are really something completely unrelated to ideas? This is the noticing of what is false; this is the beginning of self-knowledge, which is direct contact with your true non-verbal essence. This doubtful, questioning, and intelligent skepticism may lead to profound dissatisfaction with what you have been told, taught or conditioned to think. This dissatisfaction may give rise to a serious interest to find out, the intent to discover for yourself what you really are. This curious interest, this intent to watch, is the beginning of seeing, of looking, not with fear or desire or any sort of defensiveness but to really learn, and really find out what you are.

Racial identity is but meaningless information, unnecessary, not helpful and can only lead to harm as forms of conflict. Don't take it on authority from the author; just see it for yourself. The only way to "uncondition" the mind or memory of this idea and be free of it is to become fully aware of it. This means to be completely conscious of the movement of racial or national identification in the fleeting moment the idea arises. What happens when an individual silently observes it and notices it without comment? The individual sees that it is shallow and superficial, dull and divisive, limited and stupid, abstract and inconsequential and ultimately breeds conflict.

A sense of self or identity based on something so utterly ridiculous and meaningless can only produce meaningless relationships with others. Have you not felt this? As you question your belief in an identity based on the idea of race, for the sake of only knowing the truth, you see what is so. You see the low quality, the absurdity of such an idea, and the danger of identification with it, or deriving your sense of self from it. See your cultural and physical attributes in their right place and function and the freedom of global unity is already there.

How the individual is described through superficial physical attributes is entirely different from and unrelated to human awareness. This is the one truth among many thoughts, beliefs and opinions: *what you are cannot be perceived, because you ARE perception.* How can human awareness be communicated or described? Can you touch it? Grasp it with the five senses? After honestly examining the idea of race, you must feel that there is something more, something beyond, and behind all that. You are not trying to deny your superficial physical attributes or culture, but allowing them to take their proper role, place and function, no longer as a basis of conflict.

However beautiful, strong and wonderful you may feel your race is, this feeling is born out of shallowness. It is nothing more than psychological dependence, with its suspicion and mistrust. It is sheer nonsense, superficial and brittle, not the deep and fundamental nature of humankind. If you are caught in racial identification, you are in the wrong place to be free and do yourself a tremendous injustice. Are you jealously guarding an idea about yourself that has no actual meaning or significance or any connection whatsoever to Reality?

Can a race or culture perceive anything? Is perception what they do? Do they have any value at all aside from the emphasis and importance you give them through belief and identification with them? The psychological process of racial identity is merely accepting an idea about facts: your physical description or, if you will, your phenotypical decoration. There are many different forms and expressions of human appearances, of phenotypes. These are not valid bases as a source of identity; in fact, it is the height of absurdity and impossibility. The perception of your body and its physical description is one thing. But to give it the enormous meaning, importance and significance of identification with it, is insanity. You are merely describing the superficial details of someone's appearance, not what they really are, essentially.

4. Identification

What is made important acts accordingly and overplays its part. An individual's identifications are all-important and receive endless emphasis and must be protected and defended at all costs. Identification lies in all those things that are especially important to you, such as your attachment and psychological dependence on images, experiences and memories. Where there is identification, which is the importance you give to an idea or passing experience, you are emotionally held within the maze, which are the psychological walls of attachment, possessiveness, defensiveness, ownership, and fear. Where there is attachment, you need its object, you feel it is part of what you are and so it is of vital importance. Identification means you give importance to it in your thinking and in all the activities emerging from that thinking. Without it, you feel lessened or reduced. You feel you must have it, for you are it.

The idea of race is made important through identification. The idea "about" something is completely different from and unrelated in any way to the actual fact of simply seeing that something. If you ignore the facts; you are hampered. As long as your identification is related to your body, culture or other conditioning, you are not free. You cannot experience the one thing that humanity already is. See how giving importance to an idea is always self-importance, for the self is ideation.

Identification is all the words you use to describe yourself in your relationship to ideas, objects, things or people. Identification takes place when you think of a person, thing or idea as comprising yourself and accept an idea as part of your essential nature. The moment you say, "my race", it instantly becomes a thing to be defended and cared for. Identifications of the other and yourself (the "me" and the "not me") are legion, innumerable, but yet always the same, as an outcome of the repetitious words of the psychological process. The identification process occurs when you say, "it is mine, and this is part of what it means to be me."

New identifications or old, they are the same in nature and structure, producing various degrees of sensations of self, depending on the extent or degree of the attachment. The new sensation is always interpreted and translated in terms of the old, the feeling of how it feels or used to feel to be "me." The "me" always and only arises out of memory. Identification is a sensation of the self, a thought-feeling associated with behavior, ideas, or possessions. If your sensation of self depends upon it, then you feel committed to it. You fiercely protect the objects of your attachment, or sources of identification, and defend any encroachment. Identification with an idea is an activity of the mind where you cling, hold, protect or feel you are attached or belong to the idea. You are that and so it must be held onto and protected.

Identification is not freedom. What you hold, you are held within. To identify with an idea, a thing, or even a person brings defensiveness in its wake. In the identification with the idea of race, you see yourself as joined with a group sharing superficial physical attributes and behaviors, associated by an ideology called race, culture, nationality or ethnicity. Almost instantly, through association, there comes with identification the belief in an inimical environment, the usual complaining list of wrongs endured, the loss of dignity, the contempt, unfriendliness and slanders, with defensiveness and fear. You are captive and not free. You are caught in a pattern of thinking, a crystallization of conditioning, and a manifestation of the past as a conceptual framework.

Identification conveys and carries with it the fallacious sense of security and permanency. To identify is to conceive or think of yourself as being, having, or doing something that grants continuing or permanent qualities. Oh, the sensations that identification brings with it, the illusion of permanence by what seems to be the experience of the same repetitive sensations! The mind craves words and labels to cling to, as they appear unchanging in a frighteningly ever-changing world. The identification with the idea of race provides a false sense of security and permanency. Herein is an illusory fixed point, a false non-changing idea.

Yet the obvious fact is that there IS no security in life, either physical or psychological. An individual "changes their mind" constantly, but ideas about racial identification (and a sensation of self that is derived from mere words, ideas and memories) seem permanent. The past does not change. Everything in reality changes constantly and anything that appears not to change is a sure indication of an illusory state of mind. Identification arises with the desire and power to become something, yet all becoming is illusory, for whatever you become passes like all experience. Life changes, constantly, moment by moment. Can you see the fact: there is no permanency or security in life? Can you watch changing life, the speedy flowing Reality, even now?

5. Identification with the Idea of Race

Racial identity is your accepting a theory that your body or culture is associated with, connects to or has a relationship with your true nature. With racial identity come conformity, the desire to fit in, acceptance and approval. One wishes to be popular, which brings with it suspicion and resentment of all whose ways and appearance is unlike their own. Your attachment or identification with the idea of race is contradictory, paradoxical, absurd and an utterly childish way of thinking and living. Surely the awareness of your superficial physical attributes does not imply or convey your essence, any more than the awareness of anything else impartially noticeable about you. In identification with the idea of race, you see yourself as joined with a group sharing superficial physical attributes and behaviors, associated by an ideology called race, culture, nationality or ethnicity. Racial identity is over-valued; your true identity de-emphasizes its importance. You must detect the level of the problem to be part of its solution.

Yet, it is impossible for someone completely identified with the nature of the problem to see the solution. To identify with words is being trapped in the problem of racial or national identity and unconsciously colluding in the creation and continuation of endless forms of racial discord and national conflict. Being free is not to be preoccupied with or follow these ignorant illusions. Not through effort, (which implies resistance and struggle), but through letting go of the false, and allowing it to fade, evaporate or disappear.

Your false identity is the only problem, and the only solution possible is the "one thing" way, which is the way of global unity. It is the way of removing the impediments, barriers, obstacles, and ideological escapes that prevent its expression. Where there is racial and national identification, there is no freedom. Racial and cultural identity of any kind belongs to the very nature and structure of human discord and war. Racial and cultural identity is separate and divisive, breeding conflict, in its very structure. Being one thing means being of the same nature, of the same doing. Your realization of global unity is the experiencing of your direct connection and contact with each individual, a relationship with all humanity. The whole is greater than the sum of the particular parts you identify with out of confusion.

No one person is going to "solve" ethnic, tribal or national discord, which is conflict born of modified forms of conditioning. We all have to join the solution, humanity's true nature, individually. There is no need to try to change the world when you change how you feel, when you have this revolutionary change in how you think. Suddenly it all makes sense; you have this intention of wholly understanding the meaning of life. There is no word or series of words that can completely convey understanding of the totality of everything that is happening in the miracle of the moment. Even if there were, by the time you think of them, the moment has changed and passed.

Only simply seeing can grasp the whole, and in that lies the meaning, the value, the importance and the significance of life. The meaning of life is never verbal; it must be simply seen to be understood. Whatever you are free to see, whatever you have the capacity to be aware of, has its own meaning--not the words said by the captivity of conditioning. Blindness is "already there" if you are not free to see.

By embracing a racial or national identity, you become stupidly entwined victims of what you deny; the essential nature and structure of humankind's awareness, what you really are. What you truly and essentially are, your authentic doing and being, is not an idea and is completely different from and totally unrelated to idea! What you truly are obviously cannot be thought about or described. It can only be sensed or felt, through listening and watching. Only simply watching and listening grasps the meaning, significance or understanding of all the facts presented in the moment. What word or thought, which is memory and the psychological past, can describe the whole of the present, of now? What is conditioned is assumed to be true and taken for granted. What is seen is simply noticed to be actual and passively perceived and given as a fact. To be one thing with all humanity as awareness requires simple seeing wherein your being is the exact same fact as what you do.

Identification is dissolved in your serious, curious interest in a new and deeper life, a new state of being and reality. Through realization, your fetters fall way and you are cleansed and purified from the corrupting stain and abominable defilement of identification with ideas of race and nationality. What you are is living and not dead, it cannot be remembered, but is only discovered now, moment by moment. The only way to actually sense what you truly are, is by meeting it, experiencing it in that moment of encounter which is always now. Your whole, entire, total interest is in being the one thing that you already actually are, not in becoming something that will pass and that is always made of words and the reaction to them, which is sensation.

* * *

    His parents told him he was a dougla. How easy it is to identify with persons with whom one is emotionally attached and those regarded to be similar in some way! Soon he was laboring under the delusions of racial identity. It was the land of "douglas," for they had made up their own "mixed breed" designations, new words to become as the outcome of the absurdity of the identification of race. Racism is a system founded upon identification with an idea, and in their shared illusion they celebrated the corrupt and cunning content of their conditioning.

    If an individual asserts that oneself or the other has or is of a race, that individual is a racist. Can you see that it begins there? His identification was only based upon putting too much stock in one of his indelible ideas, impinging upon his seeing. Seeing was less prominent, more subtle than the thinking process, and so he thought he was the static noise of the known. He was continuously trekking the treacherous terrain of tribalism because in his identification he had already embarked upon an adversarial relationship to humanity psychologically. His deep beliefs and strongly held convictions were his cage.

    So passionate were his reliance and dependence upon and identification with ideas of race, culture and color that everything was easily taken personally and defensively regarding it. He was randomly resentful and filled with rancor over petty slights and imagined insults. His identification gave his conditioning regarding race enormous emphasis, importance and concern with its endless affinities and antagonisms. He was not in the least bit aware of what he constantly thought about, and he interpreted everything that happened along the lines of what he unconsciously dwelt upon.

    In his racial identity he found endless justifications for lunatic hate and justifiable reasons to be distrustful and angry. Like humans in gangs that shoot at those wearing the wrong colors, if there were no substantive differences he invented some so he could still hate and kill, for he wanted to destroy "them," to take what "they" have, all "their" resources and lives. He was cohesive in the incoherence of his identification, connected only to others confined and captured by the same defensiveness. Hate crimes were doubly incidents of mistaken identity. The victimizer or villain holds a fictitious idea about the other, and also holds labels about himself, what he really is. But they were the same thing: identical. The only seeming deceiving difference was what happened, all the memories and words of what had been.

He wanted to make or at least see "them" suffer for what his people had endured from their ancestors. They fact that they themselves had nothing whatsoever to do with it never occurred to him, so toxic was his preoccupation with the past. It was all he knew about, and so his memories specialized in prejudice. The sludge of prejudice seeps the same in the suburb as in the slum. The organism identified with memories, then elevated the illusory differences, and organized homicide was invented. But it was not real, for it was based upon a fiction. And the nature of the fiction was worshipped and elevated to the divine: words, language, symbols of syllables, sound, the self and thought. Oh, the sensations that came with remembering what a symbol meant and in the same instant, identifying with it! He did not see that racial identity carries with it a total disregard for the interests and well-being of humanity and creates its own difficulties.

Clearly, one could see that he was possessed of an unholy spirit, a state of mind that did not grasp the whole and gained a foothold through identification until it was cast out by understanding, and so he was not free. He wore what he believed to be clothing associated with his cyan roots, and regularly rotated strands of his hair into a cyan style. But he did nothing to establish a vital connection with his "motherland" in efforts to help them with their pressing problems, such as famine, refugee camps, infrastructure or capitalizing its economy, much less saving enough money to actually go there, at least supporting its flagging tourist industry. For in his faux identity, he could think of nothing but "his group's" acute afflictions, not the desperate needs of others. Racial and ethnic identification and its relationship and connection to war, violence, misery and sorrow were completely forgotten. His race and nationality had become a thing of entertainment with immense importance, like a fidgety child absorbed in a new toy.

He looked upon cyan people to recognize what he considered to naturally be a part of being cyan, for he knew what was involved, "how they were". But he could not see what was implied, the horrendous effects that were not only on the other side but also on the razor sharp edge of the coin. He thought heard a triumphant shout when he entertained joyous thoughts of his racial and national identity, but was it really a scream. It was the scream of infinite numbers of humans slaughtered on the other side of the coin of racial identification. The razor sharp edge of the coin was the harm and pain of war with the strife, conflict and organized murder of the "not me."

He was in conflict, wanting to celebrate his differences, yet being offended if "the other" mentioned them. He invented and imitated cyan ways of dressing, no matter how outlandish or ludicrous, just to confirm the illusion of being different, of being separate and "other", for it was a "cyan" thing no one else would understand.

Conformity was comfortable and became convenient. His racial identity was just a passing experience inside of what he really was, within human awareness. But he needed it to make him happy, to fulfill himself through it, for it came with all sorts of wants, needs and desires which kept him preoccupied about it. He identified as the thinker so he must always have something in particular to think about. What he remembered was all-important, yet he was always only thinking about what he already knew.

He did not know how to simply listen; there was always the screen of a desired or feared idea. Although his false identity did not pass the skeptic's test of actuality, nothing would disabuse him of the notion until every last particle of racial identification was examined with deep skepticism and questioning, and the intensity of his inquiry consumed the fictitious by the fire of intelligence. But he had come to talk and so one listened from the heart.

EW: "I feel that my race is connected to my body, but you point out that race is really a mental phenomenon. Is the mind a part of the body?"

BB: "Obviously, as when one has a brain injury, electroconvulsive therapy or even a lobotomy one can see that the mind has been drastically and unequivocally altered by this event. The mind is part of the body and its brain, after all."

EW: "OK, then I get it; we are all human awareness and must begin actually being aware and always doing exactly and exclusively what awareness does. I don't see how this approach solves any problem. What tangible results can be had?"

BB: "Where there is no cause, effect dissipates. The problems you seek to solve are all secondary, merely symptomatic of the underlying unseen cause. The symptoms of racial and national discord can only be maintained and infinitely expressed by the continual activity of the psychological cause that produced them. There are billions of individuals enslaved by their own false conditioning, self-made invisible shackles and chains. A clear perspective of the individual's role in the inner, psychological origin of racial discord is the beginning of freedom.

"The human essence is intangible and invisible. In the state of being and doing the simple seeing of human awareness, there is nothing that needs to be accomplished. Life is what it is and to understand it is to simply see it: to just watch, look and listen to the totality of it moment by moment. If the tangible, (which is your conditioning that obstructs simple seeing) is understood and its underlying fictitiousness seen with clarity, the inner clarity will always overcome the outer chaos, conflict and confusion."

EW: "Race may be immaterial, but if someone has committed a crime and is a suspect being pursued, the more complete the description, the better off the general public will be. And I love being cyan. It IS what I am, and if my true nature is awareness, it is still cyan awareness! I feel pain at the thought of the loss of time honored distinctions and divisions."

BB: "And you need a geographical location, to receive your bills and mail. This is a proper, actual and factual use. But the psychological identification with a region as your nationality is completely different, unnecessary, and obviously harmful. The description is never the actual thing described. We are not talking about the usefulness of words in communication about the description of a human being, for you must be able to describe a criminal to catch them. Your superficial physical attributes are simple facts as obvious as what you see in the mirror. Just like descriptions of clothes, body types, tattoos and vehicles, names, age and gender. Your conditioned culture and superficially appearing different physical attributes need not be seen dualistically, or as in conflict or opposition. They are just facts to be aware of and understood which is to see them in their right place. Your description is just how you appear to look. The communication of your physical description or regional origin as a fact is completely unrelated to the psychological activity of identification. Can you simply be aware of the obvious facts of your description without there being anything to defend or protect, to justify or condemn?

"You see the description clearly, impartially, and without emotional attachment or psychological dependency, because it is of absolutely no importance. You see the proper role, right place and function of your attributes and that they have their own meaning, which lies in the understanding of the moment. We are talking about freedom from the identification with ideas *about* those simple facts that bring with it a false sense of solidarity and a need to protect and promote, with possessiveness and defensiveness.

"The idea of race is taught, assumed through assigning idea to fact and gaining consensus through repetition. No naturally occurring facts indicate that you have or are a member of a race aside from ideas in the misunderstood psychological realm of humanity. It is a convenience and a convention created to communicate. But what a thing really is, is always completely different and unrelated to what it is called, how it is described or the known. Ongoing exposure to race-based ideas that are not properly broken down as to their fictitiousness and harmfulness is strongly associated with outbreaks of racial discord and is not supportive of global unity.

"You belong to what you must possess; what you must have, holds you. Identification carries with it attachment, or the illusory feeling of possessiveness and defensiveness. To escape from the real into illusion is to embody the false image and the fallacious label or specious idea. Can you perceive the real, the actual, factually, and totally scientifically? This is to be objective and impartial, seeing the genuine, the authentic, which is not to get caught in spurious abstraction. Being held captive in psychological activity, with its inattention, preoccupation and distraction, is to willingly remain in bondage. You see clearly that the psychological process is not real when you see its fictitious nature as a fact and not as something with which you are identified. To be identified with having, doing or having anything "permanently" is to be caught in illusion and trapped in the abstraction of mental language. The fact of the psychological process is when it is seen as the movement of the past, without condemnation, resistance, correction, or any effort to change the flow of words, images and ideas. Memory flows by freely in your simple seeing."

*   *   *

It was a university on a hill, overlooking a reservoir. Across the water, he could see a children's hospital, gleaming with blackened glass. It was homecoming weekend, and the man could feel the excitement that came from the desire to experience. The man could get see the cliques and formal groups, and the sororities and fraternities. Every possible category of student thronged: age, gender, skin tone hue, social status, weight and body types. In a school that had racial identification central to its history, there was one divided student body: standing together, yet so very far apart.

Rowdy and raucous in their revelry, there was an odor, an aroma, perhaps the hormonally derived scent of youthful pheromones. It was intoxicating to feel the heat and sense the awesome energy of youth. In the whole of his looking, taking it all in moment by moment, the man did not know if the aroma derived from muscles or menses, but it was there. The man could also sense the poor impulse control and volatile violence with its stupidity that came with youth, so he was hyper-vigilant, relaxed yet alert. The cheating amidst idealism, the promiscuity with the promise of monogamy, and the hunger for more were all there. For more was always better, no matter what the object was.

The man had seen it all before, over and over. A dentist, he had worked in the dental school of the university for many decades and had seen much. He continued to operate a separate dental practice office to "do" and not only "to teach." His dental office was on the ground floor of a large apartment building, once a hotel, on the same street the region's president lived on. He was a prosthodontist specializing in crowns, bridges and making functional jaws for bomb victims. He had many beloved patients. The patient waiting room was dominated by a huge painting of a white lotus on a yellow background that had hung there over twenty years.

The dentist was deeply orchid which stood in contrast to his white hair. He had a rich, robust bass voice mellifluous with tropical origins. A thinking man, he had the physiognomy of a very large head. Patients knew that life had put something immense in there, because he had much insight and wisdom to share. Some of them liked to listen to him talk deeply about serious topics while he plumbed deeply into their teeth. When he spoke over the riling drill, his musical voice was like a soothing bell.

BB: "Do you think it is possible for people to awaken to what they really are, and so be free, equipped and capable of making a new world for the earth and its children?"

RB: "A global unity philosophy would only be effective on children before they reach puberty or the age of thirteen. But no, people cannot do it because, especially in older people, the resentment, anger and fear are far too strong and their conditioning is hardened and crystallized like built-up tartar between the teeth of a person who rarely flosses. The deeply ingrained stereotypes promote alienation and distrust. One's response to other groups is always based on conditioning, even if it is wrong. Racism is too unconscious and automatic. Two hooded, silent orchid men walking steadily, stealthily and swiftly across the street towards you will generate fear in anyone, especially other orchid men. We decry stereotypes on the television and want to blame other groups, but do we watch the programs? Whether it is the television minstrel show or crime drama show, if the outrage was sufficient, the degradation would cease. If there was no one watching, something else must come along. And so we are active participants in our own destruction. It is impossible to forget that we have not been treated very well, although we do not treat each other very well either.

"I cringe with chagrin at the fact that eighty-five percent of dental students want to graduate without doing all the work. They feel 'We had to be twice as good to come this far in spite of so many obstacles, so just give the degree to me.' But I show them otherwise, for I do not entertain entitlement and eschew unearned expectation. They express dismay and disbelief at my refusal to consider any other way out than fully completing their assigned coursework.

"And some students' perplexing need for self-expression of racial identity! I explain to them that dentists can ill-afford to 'be themselves,' or live out their conditioned identifications, for patients expect dentists to dress and act professionally. That includes short-trimmed nails and the regular, relentless removal of crown and facial hair. I try to show them that racial identity is just an unintelligent concept if it prevents their dental practice from being successful."

6. Genetics

Racial designations are nothing more than a primitive interpretation of superficial or phenotypical differences in anthropological terms. Race ideas are but an anthropological theory, now found by geneticists to be unsound, unscientific and utterly meaningless. Faulty and primitive science has assigned a meaning to physical attributes that they do not innately possess. Humanity is so much more than that mere theory or concept, which, in any event, has been entirely discredited by the decoding of the human genome. Your superficial physical attributes are just genetic variation and nature's diversity in expression.

New gene-based technologies are erupting at an astonishing pace, unprecedented in human existence. It is a wonder that a technology of identity, which is a technological advance in psychology and a new sensation of self that is based on the findings of science (or any objective observer), has not entered the background of society. Perhaps we are too attached to this false sense of self to set it completely aside? Seeing yourself through the words or memory of a racial group, nation or any sort of tribalism, is the primary factor of man's inhumanity to man. Seeing yourself as "other" or different based on superficial physical characteristics and inescapable cultural conditioning is tribalism. In a world where the human genome has been decoded, and where the gene for melanin or straight hair or almond-shaped eyes can be altered, even turned on or off, tribalism or racial identity is the height of insanity and stupidity. Can you see that your flesh, features and shade of skin follicles have very little meaning?

The idea of racial identity is derived from a primitive and superstitious explanation given to simple, basic facts about you and made into a pseudo-science. Gene research reveals it is not scientific at all! The idea of racial identity comes through giving a false psychological significance to a mere technical fact, a significance that is harmful and insane. Racial identification carries the idea of race to an improper place and function. It gives a mere idea a psychological importance and value that is innately destructive. There is a "sense of me" given to the idea that brings with it defensiveness and conflict. Racial identification is the process of disintegration and division, the psychological process of an idea that an object is tied to the "me", and that an individual has become something fixed, secure and permanent mentally.

Genetically, physically, and objectively, racial descriptions and phenotypes may have their place, but if you are to be free psychologically, they must have no place, no emotional significance, at all. You must cease to bring mere technological information into the psychological realm, where there is attachment, possessiveness and identification. Identification with the idea of race or nationality is the cause of the experience of racial discord or national conflict, as identification is always separative and divisive. You are not free, you are limited by absurd infantile concepts of yourself and about the other; you are unaware of the whole. Yet you live, move and have your true being in the doing of human awareness, the creative center of every human being. Human awareness is pure being, not being "something."

7. Culture

Culture is universal. No individual escapes its environmental influence. Whatever your way of life, whatever we may be, do or have, human awareness of it is at its very heart. Culture is merely behavior and ideas invested in by a particular group of humans. But what is aware of culture? Although you may assert that your race or culture is real, in that they exist, any experience based on lies is still a fantasy. Any illusory passing "experience" of racial solidarity or affinity with a group sharing superficial characteristics is a delusion based upon error. Illusions have existence in the memory of man, but they are not real.

To identify with the idea of race or culture and be trapped in this deceptive sense of self, with all of its contradiction, confusion, conflict, fear, pain and violence is utterly without meaning. Your physical attributes and culture are merely there to see, as a fact. What the body "is and does" must be passively noticed, which is not to invent the psychological entity derived from identification with the idea of race. Race and nationalism exists as the word, as conditioning, as idea; it is solely a psychological malady. By your giving it importance, emotional significance, emphasis and value, you establish a relationship with this idea in terms of identity.

Racial identity and racial discord have the same root, the same core. They abide in the same room. A sense of self derived from identification with the idea of race expresses itself as a pattern or groove of habitual thinking in terms of race. There is the belief that race has value, meaning and purpose. That it is significant and important. But what could be more important that discovering what you really are, than self-knowing?

Simply seeing that the identified individual is causing racial discord inwardly, understanding how the individual does this is the least you can do. Without a cause, racial discord dissolves of itself, it is liberated effortlessly. There is no separation between prevention and eradication. To clearly understand the psychological factors that make racial discord and conflict flourish, is to be free to see its dissolution. To look actually and factually at racial and national identification is to see clearly that it is completely unrelated and different from what you really are; it is not and could not ever be what you really are.

We have all fallen under the burden of the illusion of racial or national identity. But it is vital that you get up, shake the dust off your feet and take your first tottering steps toward the birth of global unity. Human awareness is not limited by any experience. Humans are so much more than history, race, nationality or culture! No experience is what you are. Your true identity represents all the best qualities of humanity, whereas your racial identification is just an experience, and like any passing experience, it is not what you really are. It is the individual's unwillingness to let go of racial identification that seems to give it permanence. What you are, is what enables you to have any experience. All experiences happen within what you are: human awareness. Nothing that you have, nothing that you do, nothing that you try to become can add to, change or alter what you are, human awareness.

Racial identity is slavery to an imagined self; it is being a slave to your own fiction. It is a misconception of a misperception. False identification is pointed out in the ancient story, where the first false identity was, "I am naked" and proceeded into infinite forms of identities. Who said you were naked? Who said you were identified with a race or nation? False identities with their endless divisions are legion, but they are all mind-based, and cannot exist without idea or verbalization which is your conditioning. The awareness that something is a lie conveys the actual nature of the thing, its objective falsehood. The perception of your false racial identity and its source in inherently fictitious conditioning is the liberating perception of truth.

Racial and national identity has become a great threat to humanity. A change in the identity paradigm away from ideas of race and nationality towards the growth of healthy, helpful universal oneness is needed if society is to avoid an impending collapse. Now is the time to send racial and national identification into the sunset for they are already living on borrowed time. Mounting skepticism and scientific concern over its destructive harmfulness have combined to push false identifications towards the point of no return.

Reflections

One must first deal with facts, which is to see the false factually: to discover why you cannot look at conditioning factually as it arises in the moment, without identification? Can you be aware of it, simply suspiciously, cheerfully curious: just to see? This is self-knowledge. It begins with love, for you want to see that which you love. What is this self-knowing with regard to racial identity? Are you too wrapped up in the serpent's nest, too preoccupied in your false identity to notice the true one? Can you see the absolute inadequacy of ethnic, racial and national identity? If everyone in the world possessed your exact same psychological content, if they thought and felt exactly as you, would the world be a better place?

Racism is simply an ideology or system of ideas regarding race. Holding *any* ideas about race, (including the idea that you or another has or is of a race), is part of racism! The idea of racial, cultural or national identity is one of the most universally held falsehoods, merely a lie that divides and causes great harm. It is something unexamined and taken for granted or accepted as true. But is it true? While race may have some technical value, where a genetic scientist turns on a superficial physical attribute to further health, but why should it have any place **psychologically**? Why do you cling to and identify with this childish idea, while ever searching for its reinforcement and expansion? Your superficial cultural and physical attributes are merely for observation, to be noticed; not to be identified with psychologically.

For the next 24 hours, intend to see and just notice each arising of thinking in terms of race or nationalism—at home, at work, and out in the community. Being aware of your identifications and the way you label and identify others and how much you verbalize the background of your conditioning about other people or things is the first step to puncturing the inner cause of racial dissension, disunity and war.

Giving importance and emotional significance to words is felt as a sensation of the self. Through words and their sensations, psychologically "becoming" something through identification with something seen as "outside yourself" is one of the favorite activities of the mind. But the thing you seek to become, will always be just another observable fact within what you already really are, human awareness. No matter what you attain, have, become or do, isn't it always within awareness, that indescribable thing that you are? Can you psychologically become something and not be aware of it?

When the perception of another arises in your awareness, why are you not simply aware of them? In the labeling state of mind, the idea of race is usually one of the first things people recognize about one another. What depth or degree of awareness will allow for simply seeing a person's physical attributes or description without venturing into the field of the known with the associations of racial identification?

When you eliminate all the impossible sources of identity, what is left must be the truth. Inquire deeply of yourself why you desire to deceive yourself about what you really are at essence. What obstacles do you have about living your life with the true identity shared by all humans? What is the significance of splitting and dividing humanity into warring parts?

8. Dropping the Maze of Racial and National Identity

"Without realizing humanity's true nature, the individual remains in a maze-like prison of their own building. The individual exits the maze through realizing a 'raceless' state of being. To clearly see the walls of confusion in the labyrinth of mental language is the only freedom. Freedom is beyond the walls of accepted arbitrary social divisions. The individual is no longer walled-in or bounded by color or culture."

The idea of race has been given extraordinary importance due to the identification process. What the individual feels is important, needs to be desperately defended and protected. What one holds on to, one is also held by. Sense the truth of this and feel the letting go, the discarding, that brings about freedom. Racial discord cannot exist, is not sustained and fueled, without the psychological process of identification with the idea of race. One cannot exist without the other, so they are the same in nature; there is no difference between them, in an endless cycle of causation. Being psychologically free is to no longer hold to and be held by harmful sets of ideas, values, unexamined opinions and unquestioned conclusions that one has accepted as inevitable, natural or necessary.

9. Freedom

The individual's realization of humanity's true essence is the liberating factor. See the tremendous significance of human awareness in life. Freedom from what divides or separates, which is your conditioning along any lines of identification, is the essence of global unity. Where there is freedom you do not think about being part of a race or not being a part of race. The very idea of race is directly seen as utterly unimportant and meaningless. You are free because your simple human looking, your true being, is no longer impeded by illusory preoccupations.

Can you simply notice the fixed images that you have formed about humanity? When you clearly perceive the pretentious lie and petty nonsense of all racial, cultural and national identity, you easily lay it down. Can one see its utter impossibility? When you have nothing whatsoever to do with it, psychologically, as a sense of self, you have seen its danger and distortion and how it blocks global unity.

Identification is revealed by what you feel is necessary to yourself psychologically. What one possesses and protects, one is also held or barricaded within: one's image of oneself and what one thinks about oneself. *If the idea is false, then so is the identification built upon it.* The false idea of race, being the small, petty, and trivial fragment that it is, can never contain the whole of humanity or bring with it global unity. Only your realization of yourself as human awareness frees you from this dangerous, invalid, and unenlightened tether.

Identification with idea means one is deeply attached to or emotionally involved with "rational", yet completely fabricated fictions to the point of "belief". One is so identified that one can then only accept information that agrees with the beliefs, ignoring all scientific, obvious evidence that completely counters it. Identification acts as a screen or filter that only allows accepted information that agrees with your conditioning. Removing rigid beliefs must begin with questioning the false, which is your conditioning. Holding on to racial identity is the barrier existing solely in belief that separates you from global unity.

Through self-knowledge the individual sees what they are doing to add to racial and national discord in the world. Obstructions and blockages to the realization of global unity are one's conditioning, and one must become consciously aware of them. Through self-knowledge one must understand what hinders global unity, and how that illusory cage comes into being.

The very awareness of the false is the overcoming of them; you must merely see the language of identification as the false, which is to see actually, or the truth. To see a falsehood purely objectively as a falsehood is to be free to see the truth or reality regarding that fact. This seeing of the truth is the beginning of freedom. Seeing them, abandons them; you are no longer holding on to them, and they are no longer holding onto you: you are free. This is a silent revolution, where the individual finds freedom from the tyranny of their own conditioning, and the bondage of inattention through realization.

The individual's psychological defenses and barriers prevent or inhibit the natural flow of global unity. There are no barriers in your true identity, and so all tensions relax. Free means not limited by the constraints and distortions of conditioning. To be free is to relinquish reliance on idea through clearly seeing the falsehood that you can or must become something based on an idea. Racial idea is completely different from and unrelated to that which you really already are, which has nothing to with the verbal. Freedom is to be without man-made, mental barriers and limitations. Basking in human awareness through simply looking and listening, you have permanent and complete freedom from belonging somewhere or becoming something. Your freedom must be based on a new and coherent identity free from the Santa Claus of racial and national identity.

10. Self-knowledge

What of the action of simply seeing? To see simply is to perceive the illusory overlay, template or boilerplate through which one always looks—to be directly in contact with the conditioning which no one else can see for you. Simply seeing is the freedom to see things directly, as they are, without verbalization. For your conditioning to not interfere and leave the present moment alone, is to leave the now as it is, all one whole thing inside human awareness. This seeing is like when one notices a thing, such as several high value coins on the street, and does not touch them. To simply see conditioning is not to become involved with what is being said, but rather to stay with the totality of the present moment. You follow the totality of what is happening in the fleeting moment, not with the endless mental reactions, commentary and language of memory. You are simply looking when you are not consumed, preoccupied or overly concerned with the incessant flow of words.

This must be only because you want to see everything at once, to be wholly aware of everything that is happening, in the fleeting moment. You do not try to simply look, for the awareness is already there, but only and always found in the present. You can only try to keep up, which is to surrender to the moment. Resistance to life is always futile. When what is being seen and listened to is understood to be conditioning in its entirety, see how simply seeing ends identification with the movement of the past and its words. Then the subjective is watched impartially and objectively: this is the beginning of the freedom of the new era of global unity.

Then you exert no control over what you think, the conditioning is just there as an outcome of what has been and is to be simply noticed. Self-knowledge means you can only maintain conscious intent over how you think which is by your fervent desire to see. The desire and intent to simply see is the watchfulness of the movement that seeks to know or name. The snake of the past moves and flows largely unnoticed, as an unconscious process. Self-knowledge reveals that the self wants to be listened to, with compassion, love and empathy, not with reaction, identification or agreement. You must, individually, discover within yourself the root cause and beginning of all the alienation and the sense of being something separate and apart from others. You must see what identification is connected to, the unseen side of the coin.

When racial and cultural conditioning is seen for what it is (fictitious, unhelpful and harmful), it automatically fades and its movement as incessant thinking ends and drops naturally without any effort. Racial discord is not understood until each individual sees clearly their own role in every instance of conflict, that YOUR identification with race and culture is the same in essence and effect as the actors in the perceived warfare. Racial discord is like looking in the mirror. Can you see that racial and national identification is useless and unnecessary? Each individual must undertake this task through self-knowledge. This is to unburden oneself of the false measure called race and to utterly discard this theoretical concept.

11. Racial and National Discord

Racial and national identity is the same as war and racial conflict, two aspects of one thing. They go together, for you cannot have one without the other. One is the outcome of the other, like the seed producing the tree, producing the fruit, containing the seed: one thing. Racial identity, which is merely a psychological activity of giving importance to an idea, is a fictitious collective accepted by the gullible. Racial identity is harmful and incorrect social conditioning, and its end result is national and racial discord. Racial identity expresses itself as egotism and self-absorption, entitlement, supremacy, and violence. Egotism leads to separation, isolation, and alienation from others, with feeling better or worse than others and the curse of comparison. The real, actual collective and individual identity is the truth of humanity's seeing and listening, or human awareness.

Racial and tribal enmity are the same throughout time. It is all the same meaningless trouble, born of thoughtlessness, ignorance, inconsideration and the excitement of hurting people. Psychological dependence upon the idea of race carries with it that tense feeling of distrust and mistrust of "the others." One loves to blame a so-called group for the misdeeds of a few! Mutual mistrust is but another form of racial discord. Racial and national discord has entailed some of the darkest and most bitter trials of human experience, almost as if the human organism was as susceptible to it as a contagious, infectious and communicable disease. Oh, the atrocities of racial and national discord brought on by resentment, retaliation, animosity, and bickering!

But the individual's anger, disappointment or tantrums regarding instances of racial discord have very little meaning. What is meaningful is rooting out through observation one's own psychological factors of racial or national identification. Self-knowledge brings with it the perception of the connective, correlative, causative relationship between identification with ideas of race and nationality, and its symptoms, racial discord and the violence of war. One without the other is impossible. You cannot fight against your racial or national conditioning. Fighting for freedom only leaves one free to fight another day, but will never lead to the true liberation of global unity. It is there to be seen and understood as false. The focus on symptoms and the calendar of offenses is sheer futility and utter pointlessness without solving the larger and fundamental psychological problem that blocks and prevents the new era of global unity.

Inner upheaval, inner change is what is called for--not the revolution of violence or resistance, with its struggle and effort. If you are free, you no longer take part in it. If, through understanding, race ideas have absolutely no place in you and no importance to you, if you learn the entirety of what racial and national identification means and what the full implications of it are, you see what it brings about and what its effects are. The cause of the conflict needs removal at the beginning, at first. Your lack of freedom by holding on to racial identity is, at its root, merely a harmful, useless, and non-beneficial psychological state allowing infinite forms or racial discord to happen. As long as the psychological sepulcher of identification with the idea of nationality and race holds one, there will always be the legion manifestations of national and racial conflict, for inner causes will always have their effect.

Racial and nationalistic discord (or war), of any kind, could not exist without the underlying conditioning and psychological state of identification with the idea of race and nationalism. Racial discord can express itself through any individual or collective human channels that are possessed or infected by racial or national identification, and receptive to its toxins. Racial discord is merely the chronological end of a psychological start. It ends there, unless through your resistance and emotional reaction to it, you give it further life, greater energy. The actual cause of racial discord is never seen; you only see its effects. Racial discord will ever be with us until the conditioning that causes it is seen as fictitious. This awareness of the falseness of what is being said, factually and objectively, is the beginning of freedom. Racial discord is but a symptom, a material expression of an inner thought.

Racial discord is the opposite of racial harmony, but racial harmony still contains duality, the seeds of conflict. Racial harmony is still involved and associated with the idea of race and its importance. Racial harmony is not global unity. Global unity has no opposite. Racial discord must fade of its own unreality in the light of your realization of being and doing human awareness. Realization is the only dispositive factor.

Can you look at the problem anew and completely differently with an "entirely whole way" of understanding and see that we must have a different unifying approach and that efforts to correct effects will never end until the cause is dissolved? Can you see the entirety of racial discord? Can you see the entire psychological process or the source that includes the roots and seeds or causes and not just the trunk, branches and leaves, which are but the physical symptoms its effects?

See the danger, difficulty, conflict and waste of racial and national identities. All men are created equal in the sense that all men are human awareness at their core. Certainly, "all races are created equal," is an obviously absurd statement. Can you see the grief and pain, suffering and sorrow caused by racial identification? It is a snare in which you have caught yourself. It is a burning bridge that leads nowhere. In your true nature, there is no place for bridges, for there is no gap in between being and doing the one thing of human awareness.

The purpose of racial discord is to focus awareness on the problem of human beings forever embracing false identities to derive a secure, seemingly unchanging, sensation of self. Identification is born through the fear of impermanence. Through the fear of being a constantly changing movement of words, the mind seeks and invents a fixed psychological state, the thinker and word-maker. But the known was already made so the word-maker is just the process of remembering.

Can you see what the outcome of racial identification is, how poisonous it is, and how it prevents any sense of freedom? Maintaining racial identity is a dangerous game that carries with it great risk. Racial and national identity enables one to be blind to another's essential humanity. You create an idea of "them" as a separate and apart object. To objectify "them" is not to see them as individuals, but as a monolithic group, as you would view animals.

Each individual human who refuses to abandon through simple understanding their false identification with race and nationality is the creator and sustainer of inevitable racial discord and the conflict of war. The racial discord perpetuating factor in society is any individual involved with a false and divisive identity. For that person, racial conflict is real, inevitable, natural, and an expected part of life. Once this self-projected illusion is accepted, then all action from that erroneous concept is projected into actual experience. Watch the process of racial discord in yourself; see the whole nature and structure of it. Freedom is not the result or possible outcome of a mind enslaved or burdened by a false identification with the idea of race. Freedom is the leaving of that self-made prison through discarding it or setting it aside through your realization of your true essence. Get off the treadmill of racial identity, for it leads nowhere.

12. Process and Progress

Political processes and governmental interference had their purpose and may have been a necessary step, but there is no need of these if humanity awakens to the truth of their true identity, universally and individually acknowledged. Through realization, oneness with all humanity is felt in the individual's heart, not in organizations or mere words on paper. Global unity goes beyond remedying mere symptoms or effects. The individual's conscious awareness of the truth of humanity's essence constitutes their global union. Out of that realization arises spontaneous and sincere actions depicting that felt union. Then individual actions expressing global unity are easy, normal and effortless.

Political efforts move in only one direction and provide only temporary relief of the symptoms of racial identification, while doing nothing to alleviate the cause. The cause is within conditioning. The only sustaining cause of racial discord is the lowly identification with the idea of race, both individually and collectively. Humanity is already one thing. Feel the importance of this fact. Global unity can only be purchased with the coin of your true identity, which is human awareness.

The suppression of racial discord through political processes, governmental interference, legislation, and diversity programs is not freedom. Political solutions to racial discord result in the exact opposite of its desired effect: divisive mistrust of laws thrust down one's throat. The political process, with its desire, fear, effort and exercise of power, is not freedom, nor is the enforced modification of racial discord. Governmental interference does nothing to address or change the cause; rather it is merely shuffling around circumstances.

The cause of racial discord is racism which is the individual's false identification with the concept of race. In many respects, governmental interference only reinforces this process, as it carries with it the suggestion of "two things" or of one group pitted against another. A partial or external freedom is no freedom at all. Don't leave a thing as important as freedom to any so-called expert or political leader to do for you. No one else can free you. Freedom arises when individuals psychologically discard that which blocks freedom, it cannot be imposed upon you. You need no leaders to express your realization of global unity. Where there is the authority of leaders, there is dependence, conformity, imitation and obedience. These factors are all forms of enslavement, not freedom.

13. Realization

The realization of what you truly are, frees you to limitless experiences of global unity. Realizing your true identity is a psychological milestone! You go beyond a need for explanation or support of this fact you have felt and perceived directly. Direct contact is the actual sense or feeling of a thing. You are in touch with it. Your realization of being human awareness, of your felt sense of self being based in human looking and listening, constitutes what is requisite for global unity. Realization gives you the continuous awareness of what is actual and perceived, what is true, in the face of illusory projected symptoms of humanity falsely identified with the idea of race or nationality. This must not just be intellectually accepted as an idea, bringing conflict with other opposing ideas.

Your realization automatically and instantly brings with it the renunciation of ideas of identification that are harmful to mankind as a whole. Self-definitions are not self-discovery, or self-knowledge. Racial and national designations and ideas and feelings of separation and "otherness" are seen as unsatisfactory, mediocre and inferior, a mere self-deception to the reality of what you truly are. See the harmfulness of your identifications, the sheer danger of it, and the conditioning drops away without effort.

This is realization: racial and national identification comes to an end of itself, like the direct perception of facts is the total negation of all illusions, like the shadow is dissolved by the light of individual understanding. The path to global unity is a precipice, and there is only one step to being and doing the one thing of human awareness: you must jump! Then there is solely the realization of togetherness in global unity, not the effort to bring separate or particular groups together. Your natural universal bond is deeply felt. You see and find out what you are through watching what you are doing, and in that seeing is all humanity's true nature and essence. Right human relationships, the relationship of humanity among itself, must be based on what is real, actual, and not merely ideational. Realization comes heuristically, through becoming a scientist of yourself, through the experimentation, discovery, and investigation of self-knowledge.

14. Individualized Expression

The human family must allow global unity to be centered on individual realization and global unity's individual expression must be centered on authentic urgent human needs rather than destructive identification with hurtful and harmful fictitious ideas. You share the problems of humanity as your own. This sense of oneness brings with it helpfulness and cooperation in your relationships and interactions with others. Then there is a foundation for beneficial relationships, for "one thing" always has the same goals. The foundation and common ground brings a radical new potential for humanity to coordinate, cooperate and communicate, which is completely unrelated to comparison, conflict, or competition.

You are completely aware of a change in values away from self-centered self-absorption to the common good, common purpose, common justice, common beauty and common truth. The common good, or good will, is to benefit and serve the interests of all mankind. Good will is pursuing a broad set of common interests, where the needs of the relationship are more important than the individual's desires. It is not mere symbiosis or parasitism, but really sharing all of life with one another. This is to realize the one life that every human takes part in as their true being, their true essence and nature. As you undertake activities that bring a high benefit for the whole, barriers dissolve as all hands are in union for a common task.

15. Global Unity

Man is not the rainbow, but the sun. All is contained within the light of human awareness. The reign of racial conflict and national discord ceases when the clouds, mist, fog and rain of your conditioning are seen and dispelled in the sun-like clarity shining forth your heartfelt union with all others. Healing the feeling of separation arises when you are seeing what you are, and that comes with the grasp of the whole changing meaning of life, the insight into what it means to be a living human organism. Mankind is already "one thing" in its essential nature of human awareness.

Global unity is not assimilation. There are not two things assimilating. Humanity is already one thing, but this fact is contradicted by the psychological process of false identification with the ludicrous idea of race and nationalism. Your realization of your true essence moves you from the narrow and particular interest, toward the general and the global. Global unity builds a better society, as your awareness of "humans as one thing," moves you deeper within society because you are no longer living at the superficial and shallow surface of life. You are free to take initiative to build an extraordinary convergence forming the basis for working together among previously acrimonious parties in the movement of global unity.

Global unity is where mankind is seen, factually, as undifferentiated. The superficial physical and cultural differences have been seen as unimportant due to the power of your degree of realization of your true identity. As the idea of race and the psychological process of racial identification cease to have emphasis, they will wither. In this realization, this sense of global unity, you are free. There is no room for hurt feelings, fear, demands or expectations. These are all petty things of the mind. Global unity brings with it a compassion that is not based upon guilt, shame, fear or legislation.

Racial and nationalistic identification distorts and ends your relationship and connection with humanity. These ideas, fiercely protected and held to, are the chains that hold you back from global unity. In their dissolution alone, lies freedom, which is the utter uniformity of human nature. Your realization of humanity's true nature transcends all the ways (linguistically, socially, geographically, racially and so on) that mankind has divided itself. Your realization is going on when you have a deep sense of the feeling of being together, undivided. Your true identity transcends idea-based human divisiveness and separation.

Can you see the brutality, artificiality, ignorance, and absurdity of racial identity? Can you see that it is unexamined, theoretical, leads nowhere, and is without any meaning at all? As you drop the confines of false identification with the idea of race, you also drop the arbitrarily drawn physical boundaries of nationalism. Your patriotism is to the earth, the entire earth, and the totality of its inhabitants.

National and racial identification is self-enclosing. You are not free. Global unity is resisted and blocked from expression. Global unity comes into being with the realization of what you truly are, and then you naturally manifest your union with all others in your daily life. This is living in unison, already united through understanding of your true nature. Your realization of your true identity is what connects you to the arising of global unity.

Global unity is manifested when humanity's true nature garners greater attention, importance and significance than theories of racial and national separation or division once did. Global unity as human awareness is the timeless solution to the necessary relationship of mankind, one to each other, for it is ever and always of the now. You are free; free to experience the genuine fact of your essential sameness to all humanity.

When humanity's timeless true nature is acknowledged and explored freely and individually, that feeling of being separate and apart dissolves and vanishes. The timeless essence of humanity allows for no disruption or disintegration, no dissension or discord. Global unity is the new approach of real change that is innately free of the polarized debate and controversy regarding race and nationalism. It brings a note of optimism in the intelligence of common sense, which is insight out of your individual seeing.

Reflections

Can racism (which is merely individual human minds identifying with the idea of race, nationalism and culture) ever denote cooperation and love between superficially variant humans and no longer express hate, anger, fear or conflict? It is the mind of man that projects and perpetuates harmful and unhelpful conditions upon the earth, that snake of mental language that brings separation and its strife. How do you individually contribute to racial and national discord? How are you not free? What heavy fog do you bear between your ears that projects the ugly illusory forms and images of racial and national conflict? In what way does the burden of racial and national identification find a place in your mind and heart?

Quietly examine all the reasons you hold on to a racial identity. What authority did you accept that first told or taught you that? Where did it come from? Why do you want to be that? What is it you want to do as that? What do you believe you have through that? Is it because the mind needs a place to stay, that it forever seeks security or an unchanging identity to be attached to? See how the mind seeks a permanent sense of self, based upon mere words, inventing the word-maker.

Can you free yourself from psychological slavery and bondage to a false premise? It is hard to let go of anything you are attached to, that you cling to for a sense of self and identity. But like an unfit and incompatible spouse, can you let go of your unnecessary attachment when you see the pain, sorrow, suffering and danger that comes with the identification with the idea of race? Is it possible to see that what you actually are, is already equal and completely related to all humanity and that racial, national, or cultural identities can never be what you actually are?

Afterword

Being from and raised on a farm in Springfield, Arkansas, it was quite natural for me to take on the belief system and conditioning of my environment. Growing most of my family's foodstuffs on our forty-acre and eighty-acre farmland taught me a certain level of self-sufficiency that is apparently missing in today's world of looking to others for basic survival. This is not to suggest that cooperative effort in the farm community did not exist. I have many fond memories of interdependence with our farm neighbors.

I was taken to Bethlehem Baptist Church, on a weekly basis, as far back as my earliest memories. During the annual August revival week, the church had a tradition that all pre-teenage children attending services sit on the front "mourner's" bench in the sanctuary. It was on this bench that I "got saved." I was baptized in a pond of water about ½ mile from the church.

In spite of avid attention to the pastor's sermons and Sunday school, I was puzzled by many of the religious ceremonies. It might have helped if I had a father that endeavored to assist my spiritual insight, but he died when I was seven months old. I asked my mother questions about the rituals' meaning. All she would say is, "Oh, hush boy!"

My religious training as a youth had a huge influence on me. When I became a dentist in Chicago, I met a businessman and mentor named S.B. Fuller of the Fuller Products Company. Mr. Fuller's lectures were highly inspirational. He freely discussed laws and principles governing Life in a startling new way. His profound explication of biblical scriptures finally broke the frustrating shell of ignorance of my conventional religious upbringing.

Mr. Fuller recommended I read books by Napoleon Hill, Robert Collier, Uell S. Andersen, Joseph Murphy, Johnnie Colemon, Ernest Holmes, Neville Goddard, Og Mandino, W. Clement Stone, Norman Vincent Peale, Charles and Myrtle Fillmore and a perennial favorite, As A Man Thinketh, by James Allen. Mr. Fuller emphasized three tenets, "the 3 C's" of communication, cooperation and coordination. Where these are active, two or more people working together can have a successful endeavor.

The blinding fog of religious indoctrination began to lift. Mr. Fuller had only a sixth grade education, but his loving and compassionate learning came from within. The joy of liberation I felt inspired me to tell the world. Some people were so helped by my newfound practical spirituality that their support led to my being ordained a minister in 1975. My own self-knowledge and spiritual unfoldment led to embracing the teachings of Joel Goldsmith and J.K. Krishnamurti, both of which I consider to be the foremost spiritual teachers of the modern era.

My second eldest son Brian was exposed to and influenced by all of this and his first job was working for me at a Fuller Products distributorship I owned. From the age of ten to fifteen, he began conducting sales meetings and selling Fuller Products "door to door and floor to floor" while avidly reading all of the books he saw me reading. Brian came to see that much of the confusion and animosity that individuals, nations and groups express is rooted in religious indoctrination, invented ideas that have no basis in Truth or Reality.

Brian often demonstrated as a child an insatiable curiosity to know and understand the nature of things and would do unusual things "just to see what happens" even in the face of certain censorship from his mother or me. To write his first book about a macrocosm such as global unity while emphasizing the responsibility of the individual person (the microcosm) is an ambitious venture.

Brian's mother, Amanda Jane, inspired him to develop his unique talent of writing after looking to him for many years to put into words ideas and feelings that she struggled to express more clearly or cogently. Brian was his mother's secretary. She would often give him unusual books to read, and ask him to simply explain them to her, a testament to his formidable reading comprehension level at a very young age. Astonished, we watched him beat the entire grammar school in spelling bees, excel in advanced placement English in high school and obtain a full four year academic scholarship to Howard University.

In choosing to spend her last days in Arizona alone with Brian is a testimony to the beautiful bond between them. A promise that Brian and Amanda Jane made has taken the form of this book.

"The earth is the Lord's and the fullness thereof; the World and all that dwell therein." (Psalms 24:1) Since this is irrefutably true, it points out that nothing belongs to humankind. Yet we buy into the illusion of ownership. We partition and protect plots of earth that foment and perpetuate a false sense of separation. This brings into experience ongoing conflict between individuals, ethnic groups, races and countries. When you have truly and deeply had enough, the insanity must stop. Those selfish individuals having profit motives in the present system must obviously resist global unity. The rest of us can freely ask, "why not? Let us begin on that path now." Humanity's self-destruction arises from global ignorance of its innate universal oneness.

The Message of Global Unity is fair, flexible and finally fixes the problem of mind-based human conflict. This book is a step on the path of returning the earth to the wholeness of global unity. A true rebellion against the status quo is already in place as just reading the book helps question the inner past-based authority that always governs and maintains control of our life situation. Hints leading to real change will be apparent to the sensitive reader.

May the reader be encouraged to be an instrument for transformation toward global unity. This intent is only energized and awakened through individual awakening to your true identity and recognizing the true essence and nature of everyone else on earth. Verbal answers are many, but this is the only reality-based solution to humanity's conditioned sense of division and separation. Global unity is real now. Its expression only awaits individual discovery. Brian's message of global unity assists in that awakening.

Lewis C. Baskins, DDS
Chicago, Illinois
January 2015

Please feel welcome to connect with the author, The Messenger of Global Unity, at www.brianscottbaskins.com, on GooglePlus and Facebook at Brian Scott Baskins and on Twitter @Msgrglobalunity.

If you found reading Oneness helpful and useful, please sign up to my mailing list at www.brianscottbaskins.com and I'll notify you whenever I've got a new book coming out.

Order copies to give away to friends and family members.

For discount pricing on order quantities of ten or more, please go to the Booksellers Tab at www.globalunitymedia.com

Or Contact:

Global Unity Media
1200 Pennsylvania Ave NW
Suite 354
Washington, DC 20044

www.ingramcontent.com/pod-product-compliance
Lightning Source LLC
Chambersburg PA
CBHW050508120526
44588CB00044B/1763